FOOTB
EURO 2

FOR TRUE FANS

All Teams

All Venues

All Records

Euro history since 1960

Schedule including Play-Offs

© Christoph Maurer 2024

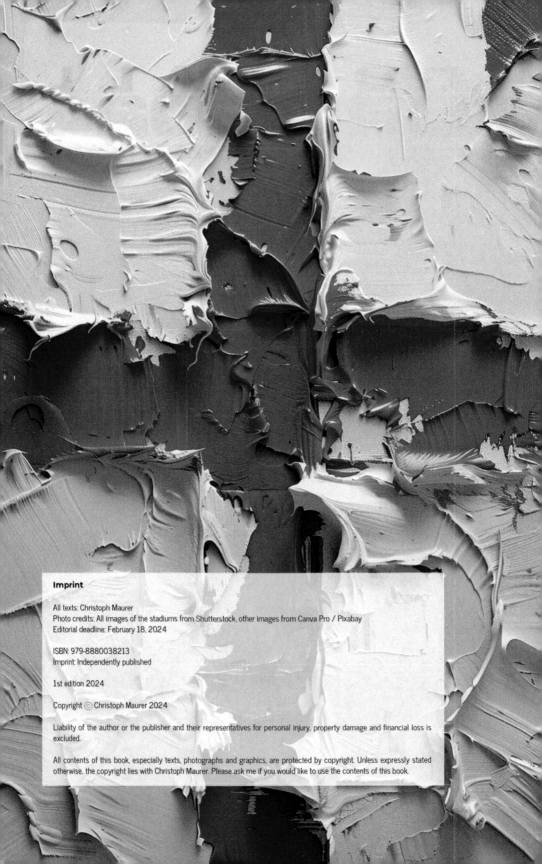

Imprint

All texts: Christoph Maurer
Photo credits: All images of the stadiums from Shutterstock, other images from Canva Pro / Pixabay
Editorial deadline: February 18, 2024

ISBN: 979-8880038213
Imprint: Independently published

1st edition 2024

First things first: When does England play?

From an English perspective, fans naturally wonder when England will play on the Euro 2024 schedule.

The first English match on the Euro 2024 schedule is on June 16, 2024, at 9:00 PM. The opponent is Serbia. The other two England dates on the Euro 2024 schedule for the group stage are June 20 (in Frankfurt) and June 25 (in Cologne).

The England dates on the Euro 2024 schedule are as follows:

June 16, 9:00 PM, Gelsenkirchen: Serbia vs. England
June 20, 6:00 PM, Frankfurt: Denmark vs. England
June 25 9:00 PM, Cologne: England vs. Slovakia

About this book

The book was designed with a lot of love for football but also with attention to detail by us football crazy people for football enthusiasts of all ages. We have researched all the numbers, data and facts with utmost dedication. If we have made a small mistake, we would be happy to receive your feedback at info.christophmaurer@gmail.com.

Now have fun with the book and look forward to an exciting EURO 2024 in Germany!

Contents

The 10 venues of the EURO 2024

The UEFA EURO 2024 will be held in a total of ten stadiums, two fewer than the previous EURO 2021. Therefore, a modified format will be used. While at EURO 2021 all stadiums hosted three group games and one knockout game, a total of six games will take place at EURO 2024 in Berlin, Munich and Dortmund.

The opening game will be played in Munich, the final in Berlin. The two semi-finals will take place in Dortmund and Munich.

Either 3 or 4 group games will be played in each arena. The round of 16 and quarter-finals will be spread across different stadiums, with both round of 16 and quarter-finals taking place only in Düsseldorf and Berlin.

The games in a group will only be played in two different regions in order to minimize the travel burden for players and fans. The selection of the EURO stadiums was apparently based on population numbers, with nine of Germany's largest cities being taken into account. Gelsenkirchen is the exception as it is the 27th largest city, but the Veltins Arena plays an important role.

The largest stadium for the Euro 2024 is the Berlin Olympic Stadium with a capacity of 70,033 seats, followed by the Allianz Arena in Munich with 66,026 seats.

The smallest stadium is in Leipzig with 42,600 seats. The Merkur Spiel-Arena in Düsseldorf has space for 46,264 spectators, and the RheinEnergieStadion in Cologne has space for 46,922 spectators. The capacities were reduced for the EM for security reasons.

Germany has legendary stadiums such as the Berlin Olympic Stadium, the Signal Iduna Park and the Allianz Arena. Interestingly, the most modern stadium is the Merkur Spiel-Arena in Düsseldorf.

The selection of the EM 2024 venues was carried out through an application from the DFB, with 18 cities expressing interest, but only ten were selected.

Below we present each of the 10 stadiums in detail. The stadiums are sorted by size. We start with the largest stadium: the Berlin Olympic Stadium.

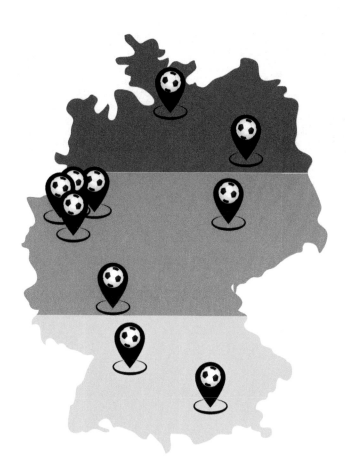

Berlin
Olympic Stadium

shutterstock/worldwide. 193497248

Facts and figures

- Capacity: 70,033 places
- Opening: August 1, 1936 (renovation 2000 - 2004)
- Costs: around 450 million euros (including renovations)
- Home team: Hertha BSC Berlin

The Olympic Stadium in Berlin, which was selected as the venue and final venue for the 2024 European Championship, plays a special role in German football history. After Germany was awarded the contract to host the European Championships, it quickly became clear that the Berlin Olympic Stadium would once again be at the center of the action, even though its history in the Federal Republic of Germany is complicated. The stadium was built during the Third Reich and served as a propaganda venue.

It regained international prominence with the 2006 FIFA World Cup as it served as the venue for the final. UEFA classifies the arena in the highest category (5) due to the renovations carried out before the tournament. With an impressive capacity of 70,033 seats, the Olympic Stadium in Berlin is the largest of all EURO 2024 stadiums.

This outstanding stadium will not only host the grand final of the European Championship, but also three group games, a round of 16 and a quarter-final of the EURO 2024.

Hertha BSC, the local football club that regularly plays in the Olympic Stadium, thus contributes to football history and the success of the stadium as an important European Championship venue.

Munich
Allianz Arena

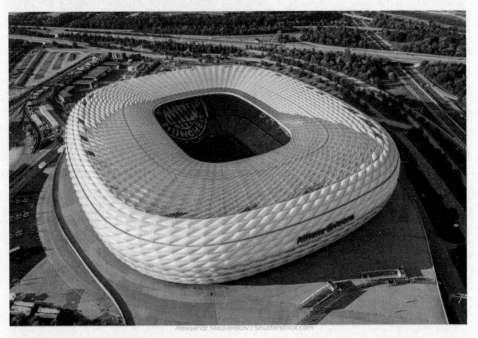

Aleksandr Medvedkov / Shutterstock.com

Facts and figures

- Capacity: 66,026 seats
- Opening: 30/31 May 2005
- Costs: 340 million euros
- Home team: FC Bayern Munich

Munich's role in football doesn't really require a detailed explanation. This meaning not only extends to Germany, but extends across all of Europe. After all, FC Bayern Munich is home to one of the largest, most financially powerful and most successful clubs on the continent.

In the Bundesliga, FC Bayern has long since achieved the status of series champions without any serious competition.
Strictly speaking, in 2024 it will also be Bayern who will take on the host role for the 2024 European Championship. The Allianz Arena, the venue, ultimately belongs 100 percent to the club.

The stadium, whose exterior is reminiscent of an inflatable dinghy, has already seen a number of big games played by Bayern - and there is no end in sight. At EURO 2024, the facility will be called the Fußball Arena München and will be the venue for the opening game of the Euro 2024 as well as three other group games, a EURO round of 16 and a semi-final.

Dortmund
Signal Iduna Park

uslatar/Shutterstock.com

Facts and figures

- Capacity: 61,524 places (EURO 2024, otherwise: 81,365)
- Opening: April 2, 1974
- Home team: Borussia Dortmund
- Costs: approx. 200 million € with all expansion stages

Dortmund is undoubtedly one of the football capitals of Germany. The local BVB is the second most successful club in the country after FC Bayern. Borussia's stadium, the Signal-Iduna-Park (until 2005: Westfalenstadion), is the largest arena in the Federal Republic and the second largest on the entire continent. Only the Camp Nou, home of FC Barcelona, can boast a larger spectator capacity.

Built in 1974, Signal Iduna Park is one of the oldest stadiums still in operation in Germany. Given these impressive features, there was no question that the Dortmund Arena would be one of the venues for Euro 2024. Not only will a EURO round of 16 be played here, but also one of the two semi-finals of the 2024 European Championship. The unique atmosphere of this stadium literally invites you to become part of this outstanding event.

Stuttgart
MHP-Arena

Philipp Salveter / Shutterstock.com

Facts and figures

- Capacity: 51,000 seats
- Opening: July 23, 1933
- Home team: VfB Stuttgart
- Costs: approx. 250 million euros

Stuttgart: When it comes to German products, especially abroad, most people will immediately think of the Swabian metropolis. Daimler-Benz and Porsche AG have their headquarters here, which means that the city is largely influenced by the automobile industry. These two companies not only provide the majority of jobs in the city and the surrounding region, but also sponsor cultural and sporting events.

The stadium in Stuttgart, which was previously known as the Gottlieb Daimler Stadium from 1993 to 2008 and as the Mercedes-Benz Arena from 2008 to summer 2023, has had a new sponsor, Porsche AG, since July 2023 and is now called the MHP Arena . The MHP Arena is one of the venues for the European Championship 2024 in Germany and the home of VfB Stuttgart. During the European Championships, the stadium is officially called the Stuttgart Arena as UEFA does not allow sponsor names.

Hamburg
Volksparkstadion

uslatar/shutterstock.com

Facts and figures

- ⚽ Capacity: 50,215 places
- ⚽ Opening: 1953
- ⚽ Home team: Hamburger SV
- ⚽ Costs: Approximately 150 million € with all modifications

Hamburg is undoubtedly one of the most prominent cities in Germany, perhaps even one of the most famous. The harbor, the Elbe and the Reeperbahn are very well known worldwide. The Hanseatic city has also acquired an outstanding reputation in the field of sport. For a long time, Hamburger SV was home to the club that spent more time in the Bundesliga than any other German club.

With the Volksparkstadion, Hamburg also has one of the most modern arenas in the country. The Hanseatic metropolis was already the venue for the FIFA Football World Cup in 2006. In 2024, Hamburg will again receive a similar honor, this time as part of the European Championships.

Gelsenkirchen
Veltins Arena (Arena AufSchalke)

Ververidis Vasilis / Shutterstock.com

Facts and figures

- Capacity: 49,471 seats
- Opening: August 13, 2001
- Home team: FC Schalke 04
- Costs: approx. 200 million euros

Internationally, the name Schalke is well known to football fans, as the club has repeatedly been represented in the Champions League and the Europa League. In 1997, Schalke also managed to win the UEFA Cup. However, many fans are regularly surprised to learn that the club's hometown is not Schalke, but Gelsenkirchen.

The name of the club refers to the district in which it is based, in contrast to similar cases in Germany where the entire city is included in the club name, such as Werder Bremen. Thanks to its success, Schalke was able to build one of the most modern and impressive arenas in the Federal Republic in time for the 2006 FIFA World Cup. Of course, this also became one of the venues for the 2024 European Championship.
A total of four European Championship games will take place in Gelsenkirchen. This includes three group games from Groups C, B and F as well as a round of 16 of the 2024 European Championship.

Frankfurt am Main
Deutsche Bank Park

uslatar/Shutterstock.com

Facts and figures

- Capacity: 48,057 seats
- Opening: May 21, 1925
- Home team: Eintracht Frankfurt
- Cost: 400 million euros

Frankfurt is one of the most important cities in Germany in terms of sport, especially in football. Firstly, the DFB, the German football association, has its headquarters here. Secondly, Eintracht Frankfurt, one of the country's top clubs, plays on the Main. The FSV is another club that is at least represented in the second division. Mainz 05, another top-class club, is also in the immediate vicinity.

Darmstadt and Offenbach are also in the area and are home to clubs that occasionally achieve promotion to the Bundesliga. It was therefore clear from the start that Frankfurt would be the venue for EURO 2024. The focus is on Deutsche Bank Park, formerly known as the Waldstadion, as the arena, and the city as the venue.

It is also interesting that the draw for the groups for the 2024 European Championship qualification took place in Frankfurt am Main on October 9, 2022. During the EURO, four group games and a round of 16 of the 2024 European Championship will be played in Frankfurt.

Cologne
Rhine Energy Stadium

uslatar/Shutterstock.com

facts and figures

- Capacity: 46,922 seats
- Opening: 1923
- Home team: 1. FC Cologne
- Costs: a total of approx. 200 million € (incl. renovation)

In 2024, the final round of the European Championship will be held in Germany. The event was planned from the start as a return to normality, especially after the previous tournament was held across Europe and the 2022 World Cup had to be postponed to winter. However, the extent of normalization required could not be predicted.

Things that are normally taken for granted, such as public viewing or fans in the stadium, will return at Euro 2024. This also applies to the European Championship venue Cologne. The Rheinenergiestadion Cologne, known simply as the Cologne Stadium during the European Championships, is one of the most traditional arenas in the Federal Republic.

There was no question that the tournament would also be held in the cathedral city. Three group games and a round of 16 of EURO 2024 will take place in Cologne.

Dusseldorf
Merkur Game Arena

uslatar/Shutterstock.com

Facts and figures

- Capacity: 46,264 seats
- Opening: January 18, 2005
- Home team: Fortuna Düsseldorf
- Costs: 218 million euros

From a purely sporting perspective, Düsseldorf is unfortunately not one of the absolute top football cities in German football. The local Fortuna is mostly active in the second division and occasionally manages to gain promotion to the upper house. However, it was some time ago that it was able to establish itself there sustainably.

Nevertheless, Düsseldorf has one of the most modern stadiums in the republic. As the capital of the largest German federal state, it goes without saying that EURO 2024 will also be held here. We introduce the arena, which will be the venue for three group games, a European Championship round of 16 in 2024 and the EURO quarter-finals. Because of this, the demand for tickets for the European Championship 2024 in Düsseldorf will of course be high.

Leipzig
Red Bull Arena

uslatar/Shutterstock.com

Facts and figures

- Capacity: 42,600 seats
- Opening: March 7, 2004
- Home team: RB Leipzig
- Costs: 116 million euros

Germany undoubtedly has a special history, shaped by the division between 1949 and 1990, which still influences the country today. The process of reunification has not yet been fully completed socially, and sport plays an important role as a bridge between regions. For major events that cover the entire country, competitions in the east, which was formerly the GDR, should always be taken into account. Leipzig already took on this role at the 2006 World Cup and will also do so at the 2024 European Championship.

However, there is a significant difference between then and now. In 2006, professional football in the Saxon metropolis was more something that was watched on television.

However, one of the best clubs in the country, RB Leipzig, is now based here and has become a regular in the Champions League. The former Leipzig Central Stadium became the Red Bull Arena, which will simply be referred to as the RB Arena during the 2024 European Championship. This will be the venue for three group games and a European Championship round of 16 in 2024.

The teams of the
EURO 2024

The EURO 2024 group stage is crucial as it marks the start of the tournament. Most of the total of 51 games take place in the preliminary round phase, with 36 games belonging to this first tournament phase. Due to the central importance of the group phase at the 2024 European Championship, we would like to provide a detailed insight into this phase of the tournament and introduce the individual teams.

Group A	Group B	Group C
Germany	Spain	Slovenia
Scotland	Croatia	Denmark
Hungary	Italy	Serbia
Switzerland	Albania	England

Group D	Group E	Group F
Playoff A	Belgium	Türkiye
Netherlands	Slovakia	Playoff C
Austria	Romania	Portugal
France	Playoff B	Czech Republic

Group A

Germany

EURO History
Previous EUROs: 13*, most recently EURO 2020
EURO best performance: Winner (1972**, 1980**, 1996)
EURO 2020: Round of 16
*including West Germany
**as West Germany

Qualification
Qualified as a host

For football experts
Three-time winners and three-time finalists, Germany are hosting their first European Championships since reunification (West Germany hosted the 1988 finals). The team is led by Julian Nagelsmann, a 36-year-old former Hoffenheim, Leipzig and Bayern coach who replaced Hansi Flick on September 22, 2023.

Scotland

EURO History
Previous EUROs 3, most recently EURO 2020
Best EURO placement: group phase (1992, 1996, 2020)
EURO 2020: group phase

Qualification
Group A runners-up
W5 D2 L1 goals 17 goals conceded 8
qualification secured: matchday 8

For football experts
Steve Clarke's side were confirmed as participants in the finals after Norway failed to pick up three points at home to Spain on October 15. Scotland have qualified for the European Championships for the second year in a row, having been eliminated after the group stage in all three previous finals. They haven't won a game in this tournament since EURO '96.

Switzerland

EURO History
Previous EUROs: 5, most recently EURO 2020
EURO best performance: quarter-finals (2020)
EURO 2020: quarter-finals

Qualification
Group I runners-up
W4 U5 L1 goals 22 goals conceded 11
qualification secured: matchday 9

For football experts
Switzerland reached the final for the fifth time in the last six editions of the tournament with a draw against Kosovo in their penultimate game. Their best performance came in 2020 when they got through the group stage and shocked France on penalties in the round of 16 before being eliminated in the quarter-finals by Spain, also on penalties.

Hungary

EURO History
Previous EUROs: 4, most recently EURO 2020
EURO best performance: Third place (1964)
EURO 2020: group stage

Qualification
Group G winners
W5 D3 L0 goals 16 goals conceded 7
qualification secured: matchday 9

For football experts
After 44 years without qualifying for a European Championship finals between 1972, when they finished fourth, and 2016, Hungary have now managed to qualify for the tournament for the third time in a row after a 2-2 draw in Bulgaria. At Euro 2020 they finished last in a tough group containing France, Germany and Portugal, but managed to pick up two points from their three games.

Group A

FRI 14.06. Munich 9pm CEST	**Germany** ☐ – ☐ **Scotland**	
SAT 15.06. Cologne 3pm CEST	**Hungary** ☐ – ☐ **Switzerland**	
WED 19.06. Cologne 9pm CEST	**Scotland** ☐ – ☐ **Switzerland**	
WED 19.06. Stuttgart 6pm CEST	**Germany** ☐ – ☐ **Hungary**	
SUN 23.06. Frankfurt 9pm CEST	**Switzerland** ☐ – ☐ **Germany**	
SUN 23.06. Stuttgart 9pm CEST	**Scotland** ☐ – ☐ **Hungary**	

Croatia

EURO History
Previous EUROs: 6, most recently EURO 2020
EURO best performance: quarter-finals (1996, 2008)
EURO 2020: Round of 16

Qualification
Group D runner-up
W5 D1 L2 goals 13 goals conceded 4
qualification secured: matchday 10

For football experts
Croatia secured their sixth consecutive European Championship participation and second under long-term coach Zlatko Dalić with a 1-0 win over Armenia on the final day of qualifying. They were eliminated in the round of 16 in each of the last two finals. Captain and leading figure Luka Modrić could take part in his ninth major international tournament.

Albania

EURO History
Previous EURO: 1 – EURO 2016
EURO best performance: Group stage (2016)
EURO 2020: Not qualified

Qualification
Group E winners
W4 U3 L1 goals 12 goals conceded 4
qualification secured: matchday 9

For football experts
Albania secured a place in their second European Championship finals with a nerve-wracking 1-1 draw in Moldova in their penultimate game. The Eagles made their Euro 2016 debut and memorably beat Romania 1-0 in their final group game, with Armando Sadiku making the difference just before half-time to help the newcomers finish third in their group.

Italy

EURO History
Previous EUROs: 10, most recently EURO 2020
EURO best performance: winner (1968, 2020)
EURO 2020: winner

Qualification
Group C runners-up
W4 D2 L2 goals 16 goals conceded 9
qualification secured: matchday 10

For football experts
The defending champions, who started their campaign under Roberto Mancini and ended their campaign under Luciano Spalletti, qualified in dramatic fashion. After being beaten both home and away by group winners England - the same team they beat on penalties to win the cup in 2021 - the Azzurri held on to a goalless draw against Ukraine when defeat held them back would have dropped third place.

Spain

EURO History
Previous EUROs: 11, most recently EURO 2020
EURO best performance: winner (1964, 2008, 2012)
EURO 2020: semi-finals

Qualification
Group A winners
W7 D0 L1 goals 25 goals conceded 5
qualification secured: matchday 8

For football experts
Only Germany has taken part in more European Championship finals than Spain, who qualified for their 12th tournament appearance after a 1-0 win against Norway in Oslo on October 15. Luis de la Fuente's side are hoping for their fourth European title in Germany and are currently level with the hosts, both with three triumphs.

Group B

SAT 15.06. **Berlin 6pm CEST**	**Spain** ☐	–	☐ **Croatia**
SAT 15.06. **Dortmund 9pm CEST**	**Italy** ☐	–	☐ **Albania**
WED 19.06. **Hamburg 3pm CEST**	**Croatia** ☐	–	☐ **Albania**
THU 20.06. **Gelsenkirchen 9pm CEST**	**Spain** ☐	–	☐ **Italy**
MON 24.06. **Dusseldorf 9pm CEST**	**Albania** ☐	–	☐ **Spain**
MON 24.06. **Leipzig 9pm CEST**	**Croatia** ☐	–	☐ **Italy**

Denmark

EURO History
Previous EUROs: 9, most recently EURO 2020
EURO best performance: winner (1992)
EURO 2020: semi-final

qualification
Group H winners
W7 D1 L2 goals 19 goals conceded 10
qualification secured: matchday 9

For football experts
Denmark recovered from a surprise early defeat in Kazakhstan to play in back-to-back European Championship finals for the first time since 2004. Kasper Hjulmand's experienced squad reached the semi-finals in 2020, their best performance at a tournament since they won the competition in 1992.

Slovenia

EURO History
Previous EUROs: 1, most recently EURO 2000
EURO best performance: group stage (2000)
EURO 2020: Not qualified

Qualification
Group H runner-up
W7 D1 L2 goals 20 goals conceded 9
qualification secured: matchday 10

For football experts
This was an impressive campaign for Slovenia. Defeated only twice in their ten games, Matjaž Kek's side completed qualification with a 2-1 win over their second-place rivals Kazakhstan. This is only their fourth time taking part in a major international tournament and the first since the 2010 World Cup. To date, they have never progressed beyond the group stage.

England

EURO History
Previous EUROs: 10, most recently EURO 2020
EURO best performance: Second (2020)
EURO 2020: Second

Qualification
Group C winners W6 D2 L0 goals 22 goals conceded 4
qualification secured: matchday 8

For football experts
England qualified for the European Championship finals for the ninth time in the last ten editions of the tournament after a 3-1 win against Italy at Wembley on Matchday 8. Coach Gareth Southgate will be hoping to do better this time after the Three Lions lost the 2020 European Championship final against Italy on penalties at Wembley Stadium.

Serbia

EURO History
Previous EUROs: 5*, most recently EURO 2000
EURO best performance: Second (1960, 1968)*
EURO 2020: Not qualified
*as Yugoslavia

Qualification
Group G runner-up
W4 D2 L2 goals 15 goals conceded 9
qualification secured: matchday 10

For football experts
After a long absence, Serbia is back at the European Championship finals thanks to a 2-2 draw against Bulgaria on matchday 10. With an impressive squad that includes players like Juventus' Dušan Vlahović, Fenerbahçe's Dušan Tadić and AC Milan striker Luka Jović, there are high expectations in Serbia for a good showing at the tournament.

Group C

SUN 16.06. Stuttgart 6pm CEST	Slovenia	☐ – ☐	Denmark
SUN 16.06. Gelsenkirchen 9pm CEST	Serbia	☐ – ☐	England
THU 20.06. Frankfurt 6pm CEST	Denmark	☐ – ☐	England
THU 20.06. Munich 3pm CEST	Slovenia	☐ – ☐	Serbia
TUE 25.06. Cologne 9pm CEST	England	☐ – ☐	Slovenia
TUE 25.06. Munich 9pm CEST	Denmark	☐ – ☐	Serbia

Group D

Playoff A winner

Netherlands

EURO History
Previous EUROs: 10, most recently EURO 2020
EURO best performance: Winner (1988)
EURO 2020: Round of 16

Qualification
Group B runners-up
W6 D0 L2 goals 17 goals conceded 7 qualification
secured: matchday 9

For football experts
The Netherlands secured their place in the final with a home win
against the Republic of Ireland. Ronald Koeman is in his second spell
as coach of his nation and won the tournament as a player in 1988.
He also led the Oranje to the final of the 2019 UEFA Nations League
and finished third in the same competition in the summer of 2023.

Austria

EURO History
Previous EUROs: 3, most recently EURO 2020
EURO best performance: Round of 16 (2020)
EURO 2020: Round of 16

Qualification
Group F runners-up
W6 D1 L1 goals 17 goals conceded 7
qualification secured: matchday 8

For football experts
Austria defeated Azerbaijan on 16 October to ensure they would advance from Group F to their third consecutive European Championship and their fourth European Championship overall, along with Belgium; In 2008 they co-hosted the competition with their neighbors Switzerland. Coach Ralf Rangnick is German and the majority of his squad plays in the German Bundesliga.

France

EURO History
Previous EUROs: 10, most recently EURO 2020
EURO best performance: Winner (1984, 2000)
EURO 2020: Round of 16

Qualification
Group B winners
W7 D1 L0 goals 29 goals conceded 3
qualification secured: matchday 7

For football experts
The two-time winners France have not missed a European Championship final since 1988. Hosts in 2016 when they lost to Portugal in the final, Les Bleus have been coached by Didier Deschamps since 2012. They qualified with a 2-1 win against the Netherlands on October 13th.

Playoffs Path A

Semifinals (March 21)

Poland vs. Estonia Wales vs. Finland

Final (March 26)

Final: Wales/Finland vs. Poland/Estonia

POLAND

Previous EUROs: 4, most recently EURO 2020
Best EURO placement: quarter-finals (2016)
EURO 2020: group stage

Poland finished a comfortable third in Group D behind Albania and the Czech Republic, meaning their quest for a fifth consecutive European Championship goes into the play-offs. They had never taken part in a European Championship before it started in 2008. Robert Lewandowski's team has never taken part in a European Championship play-off.

ESTONIA

Previous EUROs: Not available
Best EURO placement: Not available
EURO 2020: Not qualified

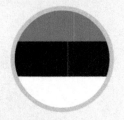

Estonia are not complete newcomers to play-offs for a major tournament. A strong side finished higher than Serbia and Slovenia in Euro 2012 qualifying before falling to Ireland with the goal in mind. The current team got one point in Group F in this round.

FINLAND

Previous EURO: 1, most recently EURO 2020
Best EURO placement: group phase (2020)
EURO 2020: group phase

Finland was hampered by inconsistency in qualifying, with a few impressive wins undermined by painful defeats. There was no run like the one that helped their historic qualification for Euro 2020, but they go into their first play-offs on the back of two wins.

WALES

Previous EUROs: 2, most recently EURO 2020
Best EURO placement: Semifinals (2016)
EURO 2020: Round of 16

These are glory days for Wales. The men's national team had only played in one final tournament - the 1958 World Cup - before their memorable run at Euro 2016. If they manage to qualify for Euro 2024, they will have played in four of the last five finals. A 2-1 win against Croatia in October was the highlight of qualifying, although they ultimately narrowly failed.

Group D

SUN 16.06. Hamburg 3pm CEST	**Playoff A**	☐ - ☐	**Netherlands**
MON 17.06. Dusseldorf 9pm CEST	**Austria**	☐ - ☐	**France**
FRI 21.06. Berlin 6pm CEST	**Playoff A**	☐ - ☐	**Austria**
FRI 21.06. Leipzig 9pm CEST	**Netherlands**	☐ - ☐	**France**
TUE 25.06. Dortmund 6pm CEST	**France**	☐ - ☐	**Playoff A**
TUE 25.06. Berlin 6pm CEST	**Netherlands**	☐ - ☐	**Austria**

Playoff A winner

58

Group E

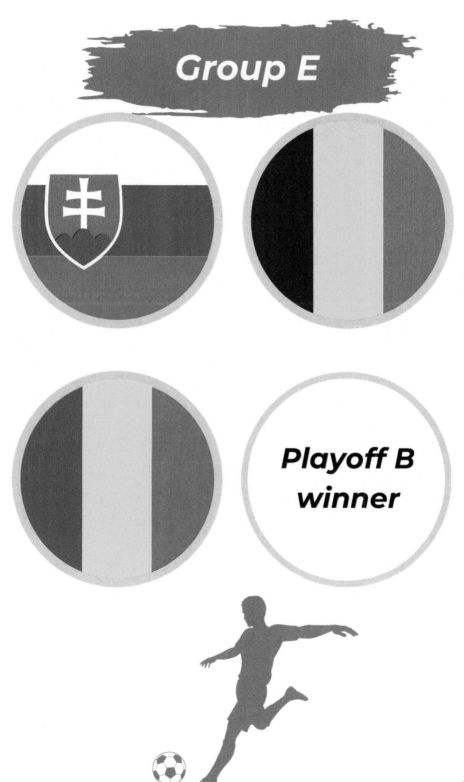

Playoff B winner

Slovakia

EURO History
Previous EUROs: 5*, most recently EURO 2020
EURO best performance: winner (1976)**
EURO 2020: group stage
*including Czechoslovakia
**as Czechoslovakia

Qualification
Group J runner-up
W7 D1 L2 goals 17 goals conceded 8
qualification secured: matchday 9

For football experts
Slovakia qualified for their third consecutive European Championship finals with a 4-2 home win against Iceland. They finished third in Group E in 2020 and achieved their best performance since the countries split in 2016, when they made it to the round of 16 before being defeated by Germany.

Belgium

EURO History
Previous EUROs: 6, most recently EURO 2020
EURO best performance: Vice European Champion (1980)
EURO 2020: Quarterfinals

Qualification
Group F winners
W6 D2 L0 goals 22 goals conceded 4
qualification secured: matchday 7

For football experts
Belgium beat their main Group F rivals Austria 3-2 on October 13 to confirm their place in their third consecutive European Championships, this in their first campaign under German-Italian coach Domenico Tedesco. The Red Devils were quarter-finalists at the last two European Championships but failed to qualify from the group stage at the 2022 FIFA World Cup.

Romania

EM History
Previous EUROs: 5, most recently EURO 2016
EURO best performance: Quarter-finals (2000)
EURO 2020: Not qualified

Qualification
Group I winners
W6 U4 L0 goals 16 goals conceded 5
qualification secured: matchday 9

For football experts
After failing to qualify for the last edition of the tournament, Romania secured their place at Euro 2024 after beating Israel in Hungary. They will be hoping to repeat their Euro 2000 exploits, where they progressed from a group containing Portugal, England and Germany before being knocked out by Italy in the quarter-finals.

Playoffs Path B

Semifinals (March 21)
Israel vs. Iceland, Bosnia Herzegovina vs. Ukraine

Final (March 26)
Bosnia and Herzegovina/Ukraine vs. Israel/Iceland

ISRAEL

Previous EUROs: Not available
Best EURO placement: Not available
EURO 2020: Not qualified

Israel reached the qualifying play-offs twice before, including in 2020 when they were eliminated in the semi-finals after a penalty shootout against Scotland. Their star players include Tottenham's Manor Solomon and Granada's Shon Weissman, while young talent Oscar Gloukh from Salzburg is quickly making a name for himself.

ISLAND

Previous EUROs: 1, most recently 2016
Best EURO placement: Quarterfinals (2016)
EURO 2020: Not qualified

It is said that some nights you can still hear the echoes of Icelandic thunder in France from their sensational run to the quarter-finals of Euro 2016. They also reached the World Cup two years later, but failed in the play-offs against Hungary for Euro 2020.

BOSNIA AND HERZEGOVINA

Previous EUROs: Not available
Best EURO placement: Not available
EURO 2020: Not qualified

After three consecutive play-off defeats, Bosnia and Herzegovina will be hoping to go one step further this time and reach their first European Championship since independence. Savo Milošević's team finished fifth in Group J behind play-off rivals Luxembourg and Iceland.

UKRAINE

Previous EUROs: 3, most recently EURO 2020
Best EURO placement: quarter-finals (2020)
EURO 2020: quarter-finals

Serhiy Rebrov's side narrowly missed out on defeating defending champions Italy and finishing second behind England in Group C. Ukraine have reached the last three European Championships, but their play-off record at major tournaments is mixed, winning just one of seven.

Group E

MON 17.06. Frankfurt 6pm CEST	**Belgium** ☐	–	☐ **Slovakia**
MON 17.06. Munich 3pm CEST	**Romania** ☐	–	☐ **Playoff B**
FRI 21.06. Dusseldorf 3pm CEST	**Slovakia** ☐	–	☐ **Playoff B**
SAT 22.06. Cologne 9pm CEST	**Belgium** ☐	–	☐ **Romania**
WED 26.06. Stuttgart 6pm CEST	**Playoff B** ☐	–	☐ **Belgium**
WED 26.06. Frankfurt 6pm CEST	**Slovakia** ☐	–	☐ **Romania**

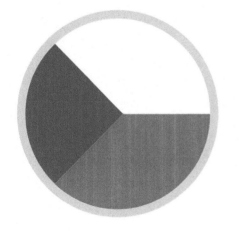

Playoff C winner

Portugal

EURO History
Previous EUROs: 8, most recently EURO 2020
EURO best performance: Winner (2016)
EURO 2020: Round of 16

Qualification
Group J winner
W10 D0 L0 goals 36 goals conceded 2
qualification secured: matchday 7

For football experts
Portugal beat their main Group J rivals Slovakia 3-2 on October 13 to reach the finals for the first time under new coach Roberto Martínez. They were the only team to finish qualifying with a 100% record. If selected, Cristiano Ronaldo will make his sixth European Championship finals appearance in Germany; he holds records for most goals (14) and appearances (25) at the tournament.

Türkiye

EURO History
Previous EUROs: 5, most recently EURO 2020
EURO best performance: semi-finals (2008)
EURO 2020: group stage

Qualification
Group D winners
W5 D2 L1 goals 14 goals conceded 7
qualification secured: matchday 8

For football experts
Turkey reached their third consecutive European Championship finals after recording a 4-0 win at home against Latvia on October 15. In their last two appearances they were eliminated in the group stage, but in 2008 they memorably fought their way to the semi-finals, where they lost 3-2 to Germany in a thriller.

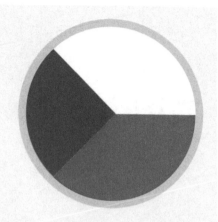

Czech Republic

EURO History
Previous EUROs: 10*, most recently EURO 2020
EURO best performance: Winner (1976)**
EURO 2020: Quarterfinals
*including Czechoslovakia
**as Czechoslovakia

Qualification
Group E runner-up
W4 U3 L1 goals 12 goals conceded 6
qualification secured: matchday 10

For football experts
The eighth consecutive appearance in the finals was secured after a clear win against Moldova on matchday 10. The Czech Republic have reached the quarter-finals (twice), semi-finals and finals in the last seven editions as they aim for a repeat of their Antonín Panenka-inspired triumph of 1976.

Playoffs Path C

Semifinals (March 21)
Georgia vs. Luxembourg, Greece vs. Kazakhstan

Final (March 26)
Georgia/Luxembourg vs. Greece/Kazakhstan

GEORGIA

Previous EUROs: Not available
Best EURO placement: Not available
EURO 2020: Not qualified

Another mixed campaign for Georgia as Willy Sagnol's side finished fourth in a strong five-team Group A. They achieved results against Scotland, Norway and Georgia, but also lost 7-1 at home to Spain. The former Soviet state has never taken part in a major tournament as an independent nation.

LUXEMBURG

Previous EUROs: Not available
Best EURO placement: Not available
EURO 2020: Not qualified

These are unprecedented times for Luxembourg. Luc Holtz's team took five wins in qualifying, which was one more than the team had achieved in six previous European Championship campaigns combined. The reward is their first play-offs for a major tournament.

GREECE

Previous EUROs: 4, most recently EURO 2012
Best EURO placement: Winner (2004)
EURO 2020: Not qualified

Thrown into a tough group with France, the Netherlands and the Republic of Ireland, Gus Poyet's side narrowly missed out on direct qualification for their first European Championship since 2012. The fairytale run to the title in 2004 remains present for a team that lost its only previous play-off in a major tournament to Croatia in 2018.

KAZAKHSTAN

Previous EUROs: Not available
Best EURO placement: Not available
EURO 2020: Not qualified

Kazakhstan had won just seven of their 44 games in four qualifying campaigns prior to the current edition, but put in a strong performance with an impressive win against Denmark and two successes against Northern Ireland in this round before narrowly falling out.

Group F

TUE 18.06. Dortmund 6pm CEST	**Türkiye** ☐ – ☐	**Playoff C**	
TUE 18.06. Leipzig 9pm CEST	**Portugal** ☐ – ☐	**Czech Republic**	
SAT 22.06. Dortmund 6pm CEST	**Türkiye** ☐ – ☐	**Portugal**	
SAT 22.06. Hamburg 3pm CEST	**Playoff C** ☐ – ☐	**Czech Republic**	
WED 26.06. Hamburg 9pm CEST	**Czech Republic** ☐ – ☐	**Türkiye**	
WED 26.06. Gelsenkirchen 9pm CEST	**Playoff C** ☐ – ☐	**Portugal**	

EURO 2024 schedule

EURO 2024 preliminary round at a glance

Group A

Date	Home		Away
FRI 14.06. Munich 9pm CEST	Germany	–	Scotland
SAT 15.06. Cologne 3pm CEST	Hungary	–	Switzerland
WED 19.06. Cologne 9pm CEST	Scotland	–	Switzerland
WED 19.06. Stuttgart 6pm CEST	Germany	–	Hungary
SUN 23.06. Frankfurt 9pm CEST	Switzerland	–	Germany
SUN 23.06. Stuttgart 9pm CEST	Scotland	–	Hungary

Group B

Date	Home		Away
SAT 15.06. Berlin 6pm CEST	Spain	–	Croatia
SAT 15.06. Dortmund 9pm CEST	Italy	–	Albania
WED 19.06. Hamburg 3pm CEST	Croatia	–	Albania
THU 20.06. Gelsenkirchen 9pm CEST	Spain	–	Italy
MON 24.06. Dusseldorf 9pm CEST	Albania	–	Spain
MON 24.06. Leipzig 9pm CEST	Croatia	–	Italy

Group C

Date	Home		Away
SUN 16.06. Stuttgart 6pm CEST	Slovenia	–	Denmark
SUN 16.06. Gelsenkirchen 9pm CEST	Serbia	–	England
THU 20.06. Frankfurt 6pm CEST	Denmark	–	England
THU 20.06. Munich 3pm CEST	Slovenia	–	Serbia
TUE 25.06. Cologne 9pm CEST	England	–	Slovenia
TUE 25.06. Munich 9pm CEST	Denmark	–	Serbia

Group D

Date	Home		Away
SUN 16.06. Hamburg 3pm CEST	Playoff A	–	Netherlands
MON 17.06. Dusseldorf 9pm CEST	Austria	–	France
FRI 21.06. Berlin 6pm CEST	Playoff A	–	Austria
FRI 21.06. Leipzig 9pm CEST	Netherlands	–	France
TUE 25.06. Dortmund 6pm CEST	France	–	Playoff A
TUE 25.06. Berlin 6pm CEST	Netherlands	–	Austria

Group E

Date	Home		Away
MON 17.06. Frankfurt 6pm CEST	Belgium	–	Slovakia
MON 17.06. Munich 3pm CEST	Romania	–	Playoff B
FRI 21.06. Dusseldorf 3pm CEST	Slovakia	–	Playoff B
SAT 22.06. Cologne 9pm CEST	Belgium	–	Romania
WED 26.06. Stuttgart 6pm CEST	Playoff B	–	Belgium
WED 26.06. Frankfurt 6pm CEST	Slovakia	–	Romania

Group F

Date	Home		Away
TUE 18.06. Dortmund 6pm CEST	Türkiye	–	Playoff C
TUE 18.06. Leipzig 9pm CEST	Portugal	–	Czech Republic
SAT 22.06. Dortmund 6pm CEST	Türkiye	–	Portugal
SAT 22.06. Hamburg 3pm CEST	Playoff C	–	Czech Republic
WED 26.06. Hamburg 9pm CEST	Czech Republic	–	Türkiye
WED 26.06. Gelsenkirchen 9pm CEST	Playoff C	–	Portugal

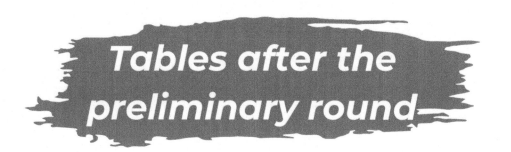

Tables after the preliminary round

Group A

1	
2	
3	
4	

Group B

1	
2	
3	
4	

Group C

1	
2	
3	
4	

Group D

1	
2	
3	
4	

Group E

1	
2	
3	
4	

Group F

1	
2	
3	
4	

Table of third places

1	
2	
3	
4	
5	
6	

EURO 2024 final round

The winners advance to the final round. The tournament is over for the losing teams. No further placements will be played. There will be no "small final" for third place like at the World Championships.

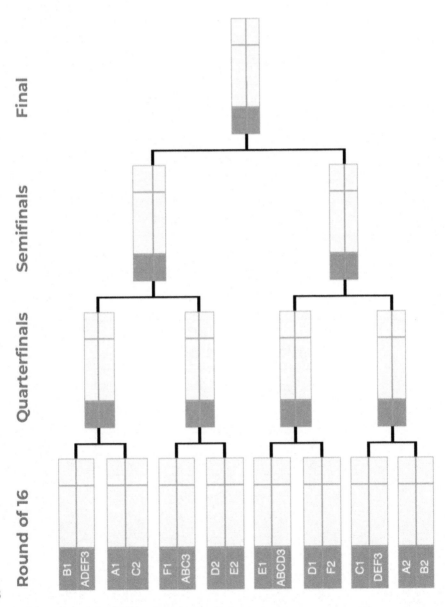

Round of 16

Sat., June 29, 2024 at 6:00 p.m. (CEST) in Berlin

Second place in group A — Second place in group B

Sat., June 29, 2024 at 9:00 p.m. (CEST) in Dortmund

Winner Group A — Second place in group C

Sun., June 30, 2024 at 6:00 p.m. (CEST) in Gelsenkirchen

Winner Group C — Third group D/E/F

Sun., June 30, 2024 at 9:00 p.m. (CEST) in Cologne

Winner Group B — Third group A/D/E/F

Mon., July 1, 2024 at 6:00 p.m. (CEST) in Düsseldorf

Second place in group D — Second place in group E

Mon., July 1, 2024 at 9:00 p.m. (CEST) in Frankfurt/Main

Winner Group F — Third group A/B/C

Tuesday, July 2, 2024 at 6:00 p.m. (CEST) in Munich

Winner Group E — Third group A/B/C/D

Tuesday, July 2, 2024 at 9:00 p.m. (CEST) in Leipzig

Winner Group D — Second place in group F

Quarterfinals

Fri., July 5, 2024 at 6:00 p.m. (CEST) in Stuttgart

Winner Round of 16 1   –   Winner Round of 16 3

Fri., July 5, 2024 at 9:00 p.m. (CEST) in Hamburg

Winner Round of 16 5   –   Winner Round of 16 6

Sat., July 6, 2024 at 9:00 p.m. (CEST) in Berlin

Winner Round of 16 7th   –   Winner Round of 16 8th

Sat., July 6, 2024 at 6:00 p.m. (CEST) in Düsseldorf

Winner Round of 16 2   –   Winner Round of 16 4th

Semifinals

Tuesday, July 9, 2024 at 9:00 p.m. (CEST) in Munich

Winner quarterfinal 1   –   Winner quarterfinal 2

Wed., July 10, 2024 at 9:00 p.m. (CEST) in Dortmund

Winner quarterfinal 3   –   Winner quarterfinal 4

Final

Sun., July 14, 2024 at 9:00 p.m. (CEST) in Berlin (Olympic Stadium)

Winner semi-final 1   –   Winner semi-final 2

EM history & records since 1960

Record players in EURO history

Cristiano Ronaldo leads the list of European Championship players with 25 games in five finals. He reached the final twice, the semi-finals once and the quarter-finals once. The highlight of his career was winning the 2016 European Championship. At the 2021 European Championship he was eliminated in the round of 16 against Belgium.

Joao Moutinho and Pepe share second place with 19 games, followed by Bonucci and Schweinsteiger with 18 games each.

Chiellini and Buffon only played one game less. In fifth place are Jordi Alba, Andres Iniesta and Cesc Fabregas with 16 appearances each, as well as Rui Patricio, Lilian Thuram and Edwin van der Sar.

Iker Casillas was in the squad for five finals, but only played in three European Championships. In contrast, Ronaldo appeared in all five tournaments.

Players such as Chiellini, Buffon, Matthäus, Del Piero and Cech were in the squad for four tournaments (2008, 2012, 2016, 2021 and 1980, 1984, 1988, 2000 and 1996, 2000, 2004, 2008 and 2004, 2008, respectively). 2012, 2016).

However, good players are not only distinguished by goals and participation, but also by their influence in major tournaments that have created numerous icons.

All top scorers in EURO history

At each European Championship finals, the player with the most goals receives the "Golden Shoe". In recent years there have been more ties, which is why UEFA has adjusted the rules. Now, in the event of a draw, assists and minutes played are also taken into account to determine the winner. No player has ever won the Golden Boot twice.

Year + country	EURO top scorer	Goals
2021 in 11 countries	Cristiano Ronaldo	5
2016 in France	Antoine Griezmann	6
2012 in Poland & Ukraine	Andres Iniesta	3
2008 in Austria & Switzerland	David Villa	3
2004 in Portugal	Milan Baros	5
2000 in Belgium & Netherlands	Patrick Kluivert & Savo Milosevic	5 each
1996 in England	Alan Shearer	5
1992 in Sweden	Riedle, Brolin, Larsson & Bergkamp	3 each
1988 in Germany	Marco van Basten	5
1984 in France	Michel Platini	9
1980 in Italy	Klaus Allofs	3
1976 in Yugoslavia	Dieter Müller	4
1972 in Belgium	Gerd Müller	4
1968 in Italy	Dragan Djazic	2
1964 in Spain	Desző Novak & Jesus Maria Pereda	2 each
1960 in France	Jerkovic, Ponedelnik, Ivanov, Galic, Heutte	2 each

All final matches in EURO history

Final round	European champion	Final result	Vice European champion
EURO 2021 in 11 countries	Italy	4:3 n.a (1:1)	England
EURO 2016 in	Portugal	1:0 n.a.	France
EURO 2012 in	Spain	4:0	Italy
EURO 2008 in	Spain	1:0	Germany
EURO 2004 in	Greece	1:0	Portugal
EURO 2000 in	France	2:1 n.a.	Italy
EURO 1996 in	Germany	2:1 n. a.	Czech Republic
EURO 1992 in	Denmark	2:0	Germany
EURO 1988 in	Netherlands	2:0	Soviet Union
EURO 1984 in	France	2:0	Spain
EURO 1980 in	BR Germany	2:1	Belgium
EURO 1976 in Yugoslavia	Czechoslovakia	5:3 n.a.	BR Germany
EURO 1972 in	BR Germany	3:0	Soviet Union
EURO 1968 in	Italy	2:0	Yugoslavia
EURO 1964 in	Spain	2:1	Soviet Union
EURO 1960 in	Soviet Union	2:1	Yugoslavia

Germany and Spain each have three titles and can therefore call themselves record European champions. France and Italy share third place in the rankings with two European Championship titles each.

Unlike World Championships, where the favorites usually prevail, there have already been notable surprises at European Championships. Denmark surprisingly won the tournament in 1992, and Greece became European champions in Portugal in 2004.

France hosted the European Championships for the third time in 2016, while Italy and Belgium have hosted the finals twice. In total, the host managed to win the title three times: Spain won on home soil in 1964, Italy hosted the tournament in 1968 and was crowned champion, and France triumphed as winner and host in 1984.

In 2021, the European Championships took place simultaneously in 11 different countries for the first and possibly last time. This was due to the 60th anniversary in 2020, when the European Championships were actually supposed to take place.

We are looking forward to an exciting football event at the 2024 European Championships in Germany!

Do you like the book? I would be very happy with a **positive review on Amazon**, and you would be supporting me as an independent author.

Scan the QR code shown to leave a positive review. It only takes a few seconds and it means a lot to me. **Thank you very much!**

Feel free to also send me a personal message: info.christophmaurer@gmail.com

Printed in Great Britain
by Amazon

40901278R00050